# A Kiss in Space

# A Kiss
# in Space

*poems*

M<small>ARY</small> J<small>O</small> S<small>ALTER</small>

*Alfred A. Knopf*

N<small>EW</small> Y<small>ORK</small> 1999

*This Is a Borzoi Book*
*Published by Alfred A. Knopf, Inc.*

Copyright © 1999 by Mary Jo Salter

www.randomhouse.com

Thanks to the editors of the following publications, where these poems (sometimes in slightly different form) originally appeared: "Libretto" and "The Seven Weepers" in *The Adelaide Review*; "Video Blues" in *The Atlantic Monthly*; "Distance" and "Up and Down" in *The Kenyon Review*; "Collage" in *Kunapipi*; "Alternating Currents" in *The New Criterion*; "Kangaroo" in *The New Republic*; "A Leak Somewhere" and "Mr. X" in *The New Yorker*; "Sound Effects" in *Oxford Poetry*; "Brief Candle" and "A Christmas Story" in *Ploughshares*; "Au Pair," "Home Movies: A Sort of Ode," "Institute for the Hand," and "Liam" in *Poetry*; "A Rainbow over the Seine" in *Poetry Ireland Review*; "Hail in Honfleur" in *The Radcliffe Quarterly*; "Fire-Breathing Dragon" in *Southwest Review*; "Marco Polo" in a small edition by Thornwillow Press; "The Jewel of the World" in *The Threepenny Review*; "Absolute September" and "Wreckage" in *Verse*; "A Kiss in Space" and "A Robin's Nest" in *The Yale Review*.

Library of Congress Cataloging-in-Publication Data
Salter, Mary Jo.
  A kiss in space / by Mary Jo Salter. — 1st ed.
    p.  cm.
  ISBN 0-375-40531-3 (hc : alk. paper). — ISBN 0-375-70499-X (tp : alk. paper)
  I. Title.
PS3569.A46224K57   1999
811'.54—dc21                                              98-14210
                                                            CIP

Manufactured in the United States of America
First Edition

*For Ann Close*

# Contents

## PART II    ALTERNATING CURRENTS

## PART III    A KISS IN SPACE

PART I

# The Jewel of the World

# FIRE-BREATHING DRAGON

Impossible, and yet I seem
to be dropped in the basket like a cut
flower trembling on its stem;
am arranged with the others by a pilot
who keeps firing from a tank of gas
an ear-blasting dragon's mouth of heat
unbearable to look at; and straight
as an elevator the *montgolfière*

lifts in unfettered calm. Silence
now, and limitless; no glass
between us and the world we clear
of nailed-down roofs and trees that appear
in the breeze to be tethered balloons.
A boy bursts out of his house—runs
and runs as hard as he can to the edge
of the yard and can't endure the hedge

that stops him; if he'd only run
faster, his outstretched arms are saying,
he'd have taken off like a plane.
Everybody's waving. All
our feelings grow keener and simpler: *Bonsoir!*
*Bon appétit! Bonsoir!* we call
fervently to our nameless friends
sitting down to a *plein air* supper.

—As if none of them had ever toiled
   to till a field; as if these rows
of wheat had never been combed by plows;
   as if the tangled necklaces
of white-blossomed *petits pois* in their flung-
   open jewelry box of soil
were conundrums we can leave unraveled;
   as if what really matters

   is *our* happiness above all, we sail
   on their wave of blessing over the sun
itself which, although hugely afire
   on the scarlet horizon, hasn't blown
up in going down. A whoosh
   of flame from time to time supplies
to our buoyancy an unneeded push;
   already it's impossible

   we'd ever assent to landing, or
   follow any command but those
of the puffed-up, roaring heart.
   Look!—far in the distance—that double
puncture in the making is Chartres.
   A worthy foil, or choice of foils,
to spar with, that singular pair
   of spires: mismatched because a fire

eight centuries ago had taken
    an early steeple down. Even
from here, the miniature blaze
    of stone that rose up in its place
is a towering flamboyance,
    and from our own we think we peer
not only far but back—to time's
    processional of nameless pilgrims

    struggling below us on that very
    path until the wheat fields parted
like gates to reveal the painted portals
    of Heaven on Earth, the saints
not yet wind-stripped of color, and winged
    Pride in fresh relief forever
falling from his horse. Once,
    people believed in dragons—

    as we began to, an hour ago,
    drifting to such a height the tinted,
interlocking shapes of crops
    became a story in stained glass
our shadow could fall into. Now,
    as if cabled to the sun that drops
off the rim of the world, we start
    to descend; the snap of treetops

snagging under our basket turns
    the stomach a little; the pilot turns
to me gallantly with a leaf bouquet
    snatched in midair and suddenly
we're kissing (as he says) the tall
    grasses hissing under us,
before we buck like a bronco to
    a halt that is not a fall.

    Still, who wouldn't feel deflated
        to see our St. George kill the dragon?
Wrestling to the ground its noble
    yard on yard of whistling nylon,
he pounds it like a punching bag
    into a flattening triangle
to fold repeatedly like a flag
    at a military funeral.

    Giddy, as one is when all
        is lost (who can deny a May
evening so visionary comes
    just once if ever?), we laugh and fill
the blanks in ready-made diplomas
    with the vanity of our names;
we fill our glasses with champagne
    whose balloons by the hundreds rise.

# WRECKAGE

Torn from the moorings of sleep
one morning, grasping not even a scrap
of whatever I was dreaming,

I realize, as I rise from the billowing
sail of the pillow, and sink again,
that I myself am wreckage

from the ship that smashed miraculously
the instant it broke
consciousness; am driftwood

toyed with at the edge of the tide,
a floating, disembodied arm
left to record the dream

it does not remember, while all the other
passengers heavily go down
to an oblivion where no

plumb line of a memory
of having had a memory
can reach. I alone on the beach

am real, and stand at last to fill
the funnel of the coffee filter
with spooned black heaps of sand,

watch as the hourglass spills the grains
of millions of associations
drop by drop in the O

of sentience that swells to a runnel,
smells like thought and is drinkable
and clarifies the thinking:

so early it's already too late
to say I never wanted to cross
into a wholly rational state,

to upend the coffee grounds like a sand
castle into the sink and rise
to the occasion of day, another

impermanent construction washed
down the drain; didn't want to dissolve
in the shower now these unseen cells

in the foam—little parts of the selves
I can't be part of anymore;
didn't want to walk away dry.

# A Rainbow over the Seine

Noiseless at first, a spray
of mist in the face, a nose-
gay of moisture never
    destined to be a downpour.

Until the sodden cloud
banks suddenly empty
into the Seine with a loud
    clap, then a falling ovation

for the undrenchable
sun—which goes on shining
our shoes while they're filling
    like open boats and the sails

of our newspaper hats
are flagging, and seeing
that nobody thought to bring
    an umbrella, puts

up a rainbow instead.
A rainbow over the Seine,
perfectly wrought as a draw-
    bridge dreamed by a child

in crayon, and by the law
of dreams the connection
once made can only be lost;
    not being children

we stand above the grate
of the Métro we're not
taking, thunder underfoot, and
soak up what we know:

the triumph of this *arc-
en-ciel,* the dazzle
of this monumental
prism cut by drizzle, is

that it vanishes.

# A Leak Somewhere

No toy in a bathtub, the Titanic;
but on our twenty-one-inch screen
it's faintly laughable, as Barbara Stanwyck
and her daughter in their lifeboat gasp
at the sight of the great vessel sliding
into the North Atlantic like a spoon.

Yet only faintly laughable.
When the ship blows up, with Stanwyck's son
and husband on it, the four of us
(warm beneath one blanket flung
across a comfy sofa in
the lifeboat of our living room)

bob with the waves of melodrama.
How ironic!  Their family had split
even onboard, but along other lines:
living abroad had spoiled the girl
(Annette was so pretentious she
addressed her fellow Yanks in French),

but Norman, with his normal name,
might still be saved in Michigan.
Or that was Stanwyck's plan.  And now
he's sinking with shallow Clifton Webb,
his Paris-besotted father, to
a depth where such distinctions are all

for naught.  The ship's a symbol of
society, we tell our children—
belowdecks, into the porthole maws
of furnaces, bare-torsoed men
stoke coal until their sweat runs black;
when the iceberg slices through the hull,

they're flooded in an instant. Above
in steerage, the crammed-in families
of the kerchiefed, overexcitable poor
race for the door and, as water climbs,
scramble upstairs where Guggenheims
and Astors (so well-bred they barely

raise an eyebrow even for
historic personal disasters)
set down their hands of bridge, and don
life jackets like the latest fashion.
Not enough lifeboats?  Noblesse oblige,
everybody at once is noble,

and an instinctive revolution
reshuffles the classes: women and children
first.  Down the Jacob's ladder
of rope they struggle to the shaky
safety of going on living, while
those left behind on the heavenly

height of the tilting ship take solace
in their perfectly rehearsed rendition
of "Nearer, My God, to Thee."
Oh, you and I can laugh.  But having
turned off the set, and led the kids
upstairs into dry beds, we sense

that hidden in the house a fine
crack—nothing spectacular,
only a leak somewhere—is slowly
widening to claim each of us
in random order, and we start to rock
in one another's arms.

# VIDEO BLUES

My husband has a crush on Myrna Loy,
and likes to rent her movies, for a treat.
It makes some evenings harder to enjoy.

The list of actresses who might employ
him as their slave is too long to repeat.
(My husband has a crush on Myrna Loy,

Carole Lombard, Paulette Goddard, coy
Jean Arthur with that voice as dry as wheat . . .)
It makes some evenings harder to enjoy.

Does he confess all this just to annoy
a loyal spouse?  I know I can't compete.
My husband has a crush on Myrna Loy.

And can't a woman have her dreamboats? Boy,
I wouldn't say my life is incomplete,
but some evening I could certainly enjoy

two hours with Cary Grant as *my* own toy.
I guess, though, we were destined not to meet.
My husband has a crush on Myrna Loy,
which makes some evenings harder to enjoy.

# BRIEF CANDLE

The funicular, effortless
as a toy, glides humming to a stop
halfway uphill.  Buzzing with tourists, the steps
break, halfway again, at a terrace
where we pause to catch our breath, and half of Paris.

But today, in the August haze,
the view from Montmartre is just the odd
tin rooftop the sun's dropped match sets ablaze,
the gilded dome of Les Invalides,
the pipe dream of the Pompidou.  Should these

not do, dozens of tiny,
tin Eiffel Towers glint at our feet,
each the capital of repeating shapes
on the map of a vendor's Persian carpet.
Balloon-sellers too, a bongo group, a *triste*

untalented guitarist—
we rise above them all to enter
buoyantly the dark of Sacré-Coeur.
Christ is still grandly aflame
behind the altar, his heart of gold

mosaic flickering
with feeling, his outflung arms
in a gesture that serves for love and crucifixion.
And in unison, a hundred hands
reach for candles and a pocketful of change.

But now a half-blind mob
   behind them is advancing, afraid
the candelabra, tiered like Christmas trees,
   have no room left for one last prayer.
A boy sets *his* taper on top (being the star

      to him seems natural),
   while a girl illumines hers, a can
of Coke aloft in the other hand.  All
   for nothing: how in the world had we missed
the man whose job is to snuff our wishes out?

      That's how space is found:
   the instant people turn around,
he picks their candles up by the blazing wicks,
   two-fisted, and with blackened thumbs
chucks them into a pail—then the next soul comes,

      paying fifteen francs
   for the longest kind, which lasts the same
as for people who paid five, or who never came.
   Could it be he enjoys this? Or does
he stand there for a divine indifference

      to all our pleas and thanks
   and the guttering hope we matter?  Though
an arrow points the *Sens de la visite,*
   we decide to make our own sense of it
outdoors, in the all-consuming furnace of summer.

          And halfway down the steps
     again, we run into a gypsy
beggar of five or six, who has set up shop
     on a step.  His cup is empty,
its earnings slipped beneath his rug, or rag,

          but he hasn't hid his booty
     of big, dirty biscuits, embossed like coins,
which triple as money, food, and toys at once.
     From his hands, themselves as sooty
as the man's upstairs, they rise in fragile towers

          he demolishes carefully, and over and over.

# Up and Down

### 1. *A Magnet*

Since she was two, it had held up her end
on the door of the fridge: a plywood magnet stamped
with the fingerpainted imprint of her hand.
Essence-of-kid, all cheerfulness, in a pure
nursery red, it stood for her signature
and seemed, back then, to raise itself in greeting.

When was it that it started to wave goodbye?
One day some sort of scrap it had always kept
in lofty view—report card, shopping list,
snapshot of somebody's new baby—slipped
with it, cinematically, down the door
like a climber's grip, failing along a rock face.

—Demagnetized, of course, by the very years
that made her real hands strong.  I've placed it high,
supporting nothing weightier than itself,
against that time I'd sense in me a fainter
grasp on the little girl who never crossed
the street without my finger in her fist.

### 2. *A Swing*

A rope swing, hung from a tree—
         and you've easily gone a mile
by now, your arc of flight
         retracing a broad smile
as you swoop down to me.
         I'm not supposed to touch;

only to face you while
        you call commands, like "Watch!"

But it's you who ought to look,
        this morning, where we are.
We're in the middle of France,
        in the town of Sainte-Sévère,
in a province called Berry;
        your makeshift *balançoire*
is sweeping through a sky
        that's bluer because a duke

in the fourteenth century
        illumined the *très riches heures*—
or others did it for him
        while sitting very still.
That's not to say *you* will;
        but didn't you even hear
how, perfectly in time
        with your pumping, a church bell

began to chime and clang?
        Well, you're the very clapper
in the middle of the world
        and can't be asked to stop.
I'll tell you about it later.
        For now, keep reaching up
and let your soul swing free
        as a bell with a foreign tongue.

# Home Movies: A Sort of Ode

Because it hadn't seemed enough,
after a while, to memorialize
more Christmases, the three-layer cakes
ablaze with birthday candles, the blizzard
Billy took a shovel to,
Phil's lawn mower tour of the yard,
the tree forts, the shoot-'em-ups
between the boys in new string ties
and cowboy hats and holsters,
or Mother sticking a bow as big
as Mouseketeer ears in my hair,

my father sometimes turned the gaze
of his camera to subjects more
artistic or universal:
rapt close-ups of a rose's face;
a real-time sunset (nearly an hour);
what one assumes were brilliant autumn
leaves before their colors faded
to dry beige on the aging film;
a great deal of pacing, at the zoo,
by polar bears and leopards caged,
he seemed to say, like him.

What happened between him and her
is another story. And just as well
we have no movie of it, only
some unforgiving scowls she gave
through terrifying, ticking silence
when he must have asked her (no
sound track) for a smile.
Yet the scenes I keep reversing to

are private: not those generic cherry
blossoms at the full, or the brave
daffodil after a snowfall;

instead, it's the re-run surprise
of the unshuttered, prefab blanks
of windows at the back of the house,
and how the lines of aluminum
siding are scribbled on with meaning
only for us who lived there.
It's the pair of elephant bookends
I'd forgotten, with the upraised trunks
like handles, and the books they sought
to carry in one block to a future
that scattered all of us.

And look: it's the stoneware mixing bowl
figured with hand-holding dancers
handed down so many years
ago to my own kitchen, still
valueless, unbroken. Here
she's happy, teaching us to dye
some Easter eggs in it, a Grecian
urn of sorts near which—a foster
child of silence and slow time
myself—I smile because she does,
and patiently await my turn.

# LIBRETTO

*Libretto.* That's the first Italian word
    she wants to teach me: "little book."
This afternoon (but why are we alone?
    Were Daddy and my brothers gone
all day, or has memory with its flair
    for simple compositions air-
brushed them from the shot?) she's set aside
    just for the two of us, and a lesson.

On an ivory silk couch that doesn't fit
    the life she's given in Detroit,
we gaze across the living room at the tall
    "European" drapes she's sewn
herself: a work of secret weights and tiers,
    hung after cursing at her own
mother's machine.  She lets the needle fall
    onto the record's edge; then turns

to pull a hidden cord, and the curtain rises
    on Puccini's strings and our front view
of shut two-car garages, built for new
    marriages constructed since the war.
Well, not so new.  It's 1962
    and though I'm only eight, I know
that with two cars, people can separate.
    He went away; came back for more

operatic scenes heard through the wall
    as if through a foreign language.  Muffled
fury and accusation, percussive sobs:

they aren't happy.  Who couldn't tell
without the words? *Libretto*. On my knees
    the English text, the Italian on hers,
and a thrill so loud the coffee table throbs.
    I'm following her finger as

we're looping to a phrase already sung
    or reading four lines at a time
of people interrupting and just plain
    not listening, and yet the burden
of the words is simple: Butterfly must die.
    Pinkerton will betray her, though the theme
rippling above him like a hoisted flag
    is The Star-Spangled Banner.  Mother, why

would a Japanese and an American
    sing Italian at each other?
Why would he get married and not stay?
    And have a child he'd leave to wait
with the mother by the screen with her telescope
    for the ship of hope?  Why, if he knew
it wouldn't last, did he come back to Japan?
    —But I'm not asking her. *That's men*

is her tacit, bitter answer; was always half
    her lesson plan. *O say, can you see . . .*
yes, now I can.  Your dagger's at the throat
    and yet I feel no rage; as tears
stream down our faces onto facing pages
    fluttering like wings, I see you meant

like Butterfly to tie a blindfold over
    a loved child's eyes: the saving veil of Art.

For it is only a story.  When the curtain
    drops, our pity modulates
to relief she isn't us, and what's in store
    for you, divorce and lonely death,
remains distant.  We have our nights to come
    of operas to dress up for,
our silly jokes, our shopping, days at home
    when nothing is very wrong and in my chair

I read some tragedy in comfort, even
    a half-shamed joy. You gave me that—
my poor, dear parents, younger then than I
    am now; with a stagestruck, helpless wish
that it wouldn't hurt and that it would, you made
    me press my ear against the wall
for stories that kept me near and far,
    and because the hurt was beautiful

even to try to write them; to find that living
    by stories is itself a life.
Forgive whatever artifice lies
    in my turning you into characters
in my own libretto—one sorry hand
    hovering above the quicksand
of a turntable in a house in Detroit
    I can't go back to otherwise.

# SOUND EFFECTS

## LOUIS MACNEICE, 1907–1963

If every death's an echo
of some hand-picked theme
struck from the tuning fork
at birth, one may as well
first backtrack to a cave
he knew in County Wicklow,

hidden so cleverly
in the side of Knockagh Hill
that, homing as a man,
he had to walk full circle
before he found its mouth.
Obscurely in the den

of memory his mother
told him to be brave,
though they took away her womb,
then locked away her grief
in a Dublin clinic, where
bacteria with that knack

for the random knocked on doors
until she opened hers.
He dove into the cave
of his bedsheets when they told him
and made a sort of grave
a guilty boy could rise from.

If every death's an echo,
think of his widowed father
leading the children down
the underground cathedral
of salt mines, "caves of crystal
and man-made thunder,"

as workmen armed with picks
quarried such queer music
from the labyrinthine walls—
gorgeously distorted
from however it had started
in a poet's chambered ears.

Knock knock—he'll never wake—
on his door at Oxford where
he read by the flickering fire
of Plato's cave that all
we know is shadow, or
the echo of a shadow;

where buried in the measures
of Coleridge he came
to the sunless sea and caverns
measureless to man,
and plumbed them to the bottom
of the page where a visitor

from Porlock knocked and stuck
a footnote in the door.
That sent him to the taverns
where dreams came by the dram
and in the smoke-dimmed light
he raised his glass like a torch.

And wrote play after play
for the disembodied voices
that groped within the grotto
of the radio and vanished
when someone else from Porlock
switched the era off—

about the time his script
"Persons from Porlock" called
him underground to tape
some waterfall effects,
in a cave lined like a lung
with damp he couldn't take.

Master of the refrain
that rang and rang and wrung
your heart out when it gave
its echoes somewhat wrong,
thinking he was brave
he strolled back in the rain.

# CUTLERY

On my lapel there's a pin
(truth to tell, three-in-one)
of a fork, knife, and spoon,
each the length of a life-sized tine.
I like to wear them when
I go out to dine,

and they rarely fail
to call up a delighted squeal:
because they aren't real?
Because they are, though small?
In the doll's house of art, the table
is always set and a meal

deliciously out of the question.

# HAIL IN HONFLEUR

All of a sudden, hail
fell out of the sky and hopped
    like popcorn in the pan,
hail hobbled us as we ran
    across the cobblestones

    into a restaurant
where a portly couple sat
    at a window with an ideal
view of the hail-pocked port,
    though each was more content
examining the sails
    in steaming bowls of mussels.

    He was securely tied
and jacketed and vested;
    she solemnly big-breasted,
her tight suit in a bright
    blue you'd never see
in Paris these days, unless
    on a wall, in a Raoul Dufy.

    Hail piled up in the street
like the shaved ice where a fish-
    monger beds his fish,
but indoors was more to eat:
    tiered platters of *fruits de mer*
consumed their attention for
    at least another hour,

and the pair of them looked up
not once nor took a pause
    from extracting the last flakes
from a pair of lobster claws.
    Well, having come for soup
and shelter only, we
    could stare no more, and wondered,

    should we try to hail a cab?
But the hail came to a halt
    and turned to a fine-grained sugar
just as they were about
    to start their *tarte Tatin.*

# The Jewel of the World

*1.*

Lion and unicorn, with as sure
a sense of theater as saints
in paintings who flank Mary's throne,

or as circus animals
on hind legs—one paw wrapped around
a flagpole while another lifts

the curtain of a curious tent
paisleyed with golden, swimming tears—
open the magnificent

tapestry of a landscape rising
impossibly backstage in red:
a floral vertigo that rabbits

munch on in mid-air, while goats
and dogs and spread-winged falcons float
above the perennial thought of green.

Four trees planted in the ocean-
blue of the Lady's island spring
up like four seasons all at once

and forever. Flowering orange and oak,
holly and pine: each of them,
like her, is in its prime.

Set like a jewel in the oval
ring of her island, fabulous
in her studded headdress

(in the fashion of the day,
one stiff lock of braided hair
shoots up like a horn), the Lady

holds, in a kind of winding-sheet,
a necklace to be buried in
the casket in her servant's hands.

Gone is the life of senses she
had always kept in fine control;
she casts it off to save her soul.

But like a miniature of the trunk
a magician asks his volunteer
to enter so she may be sawn

in half, the jewel box leaves open
questions of renunciation.
Who could give away the world

undivided? Or at least
this one, a blooming hyperbole
of earthly beauty? A MON SEUL

DESIR, the legend reads above
her tent, which only makes it clear
that the desire to want no more

has always been too much to want.
We've kept this jewel of tapestry—
and swear she puts the necklace on.

2.

Step out from the Cluny and cross the Seine.
The bells are floating at Notre Dame, where sun
throws patterns from the scaffolding and swims
blind into the windows where it can.
The perpetual rose grows dirty and is cleaned
but never sheds a petal.

Nor, when you walk west along the quai,
watching the river splinter into stains
of painful brilliance, on to where the joined
pyramid of glass above the Louvre
flashes its hand, a diamond marrying
buried years to this one, will you find

a single way to turn your face from life—
nowhere in the museum's honeycomb
of centuries. There, within one niche
eternity gives to Titian, his *La mise
en tombeau* is lowering the priceless
body into its unseen vault again:

Jesus Christ, King of the Jews, the jewel
of the world. Held still by his ring
of mourners in a winding-sheet, his weight
is nearly more than anyone can bear.
Heaven and Earth. Son of God in eclipse,
head and torso blocked off by the shadow

cast by an enigma: Nicodemus,
Joseph of Arimathea, John the Baptist
half-seem to be lifting him into the light.
Going or coming? Mary Magdalene knows
nothing yet, as she turns the Virgin away,
of visions meant for her on the third day—

the stone gone from the sepulchre, the angels
waiting at head and foot, the man she weeps for
unrecognized until he speaks her name.
The story hangs from his suspended frame
only because we know it; have seen him rise
in other galleries, stepping from each tomb

as if from a refreshing bath.
Prolific Titian lovingly stroked more
farewells like these in light and shadow,
Christ's head at the right, then at the left;
one ends up at the Louvre, two at the Prado,
the world abloom with entombments.

3.

In Venice, sinking imperceptibly
each morning as the sun climbs from a sea
whose iridescence flakes into mosaics,

Titian has risen once again and turns
to his final canvas, the massive *Pietà*
meant for an altarpiece near his own grave.

Fierce Mary Magdalene, having cast off
her sinner's finery—even the jeweled tones
borrowed from Bellini—runs in, a smear

of army green descending from the left,
arm raised in grief, half as if she'd wave
us in and half away. What's to be done,

while the Virgin cradles uselessly the grown
son in her lap, but kneel to her and pray
(as does half-naked, ragged St. Jerome

or Job or Nicodemus or perhaps
Joseph of Arimathea—an old man,
in any case, identified as Titian)

and stare into the face of all our losses?
The master drops his brush, paints with bare hands.
Pearl of the late style, the head of Jesus

reclines into the lustrous oyster shell
of the temple apse, colder than the deepest
place in the ocean, a face so radiantly

cold, so terrifying, even Mary
holds him at a distance.
Titian also has a favorite son.

He has propped a votive panel—a little painting
within a painting, of Orazio
praying with his father—against one

of the pedestals with lions' faces raising
Moses and the Hellespontic sibyl,
two prophets, to the level of the saints,

and under the cross-bearing sibyl's robes
has placed, horrifically, what even he
can't wholly comprehend: a severed hand.

Suspend your disbelief. It is the hand
passed on to Palma, who'll finish the *Pietà*
after Titian and his son fall to the plague.

Palma lifts the brush much like a needle
saving a dropped stitch, so that each thread
in the tapestry of loss is duly numbered,

much as the Lord counts hairs on every head
before he claims us, much as the attorney
catalogues, when thieves ransack the house

after Titian's death, what now exists
elsewhere: they took away, he writes, "things
of gold, silver and gems,

and innumerable paintings of great value."

# Distance

From up here, the insomniac
   river turning in its bed
  looks like a line somebody painted
      so many years ago it's hard
to believe it was ever liquid; a motorboat
   winks in the sun and leaves a wake
that seals itself in an instant, like the crack
         in a hardly broken heart.

And the little straight-faced houses
      that with dignity bear the twin
   burdens of being unique and all alike,
      and the leaf-crammed valley like the plate
of days that kept on coming and I ate
   though laced with poison: I can look
over them, from this distance, with an ache
         instead of a blinding pain.

Sometimes, off my guard, I half-
      remember what it was to be
   half-mad: whole seasons gone; the fear
      a stranger in the street might ask
the time; how feigning normality
   became my single, bungled task.
What made me right again? I wouldn't dare
         to guess; was I let off

for good behavior? Praise
to whatever grace or power preserves
the living for living . . . Yet I see the square
down there, unmarked, where I would pace
endlessly, and as the river swerves
around it, wonder what portion of
love I'd relinquish to ensure
I'd never again risk drowning.

# PART II

# Alternating Currents

*To the memory of the real, ideal Sherlock Holmes*
JEREMY BRETT
1935–1995

# ALTERNATING CURRENTS

### 1. *Reading in the Dark*

Imagine, if you will, a hotel
room fronting Niagara Falls. Helen
Keller has been brought here by
her teacher, Annie Sullivan,
to meet their good friend Dr. Bell,
inventor of the telephone,
who has long worked with the deaf.
Helen, thirteen, already known
around the world for having thirsted
at the well of knowledge in her own
backyard, where Sullivan had spilled
water in one hand and spelled
the word into the other, now
lets him lift her hand in his
like a receiver, and gently press
it flat against the window's ear.

The glass is cold. And through her splay
fingers a liquid thunderbolt
of vibration charges and discharges
at once, so thrilling in its force
that she nearly tastes the spray—
though, one must add, the girl is made
of words more than of anything
by now; she feels what she's been told.

Teacher gave her half the world
she knows. How to fathom, then,
the ingratitude that surfaces
in dreams? At Radcliffe, later, where

Teacher sits through every class
and unabsorbedly (for she's
a medium, a conductor, and what
greater sacrifice?) transmits
directly to her charge's hand
all the professors' lectures, she
appears sometimes in Helen's nightmares
as a quarrelsome tormentor,
driving her to "an abyss, a perilous
mountain pass or rushing torrent."
Once "I saw her robed in white
on the brink of Niagara Falls."
Her costume seemed to be an angel's.
When she dropped into the whirlpool,
Helen, frantic, dove in to pull
Teacher from danger; the figure wrestled
out of her arms and swam to shore
untwinned. And this—the unthinkable
thoughtlessness of one who loved her—
was the purest terror.

   But how lucky she is! Instead of toys
they bring her famous men: William
James, W. E. B. Du Bois,
Oliver Wendell Holmes, Mark Twain.
One day she'll touch Caruso's voice.
Somebody in Gardiner, Maine
has named a lumber vessel for her.
Hers is a fate that launched a ship.
At her fingertips, the Braille
armies of words amass: she scans
*The Iliad* in the original.

(What is original? She hasn't
dared to ask since, at eleven,
a story she had thought she thought
up wholly by herself had proven
to be the tale of a "plagiarist.")
Sometimes she is just as glad
not to tire Teacher, and will work
late into the night—but then,
she writes to kindly Mrs. Hutton,
"one wearies of the clash of spears
and the din of battle." No one hears
the punctured pages turning as
she soldiers on alone, the blind
reading the blind: the lovely Helen
following Homer in the dark.


2. *The Final Problem*

    Across the ocean, an oculist,
Dr. Arthur Conan Doyle,
plots the ultimate crime. He boasts
to his mother, "I think of slaying Holmes . . .
& winding him up for good and all.
He takes my mind from better things."
Twirling the weapon in his hand,
he pens the title: "The Final Problem."

    Deflecting blame, perhaps, he sets
the end on foreign soil. A train
of reasoning takes Holmes and Watson
to Switzerland, fleeing that regal
rival, the "Napoleon

of crime," the spider in a vile
network of radiating evil.
(Too bad. Had Conan Doyle more art, he
would have created Moriarty
long before.) Face to face
at last, detective and nemesis—
their twin defiance heightened by
the pointed altitude of the Alps—
peer at each other in a bliss
of imminence. The great men tumble
in a wrestler's grip together
down the Reichenbach Fall—unseen
by Watson, who runs up too late.
Yes, that's very good. He'll call
helplessly down the abyss
to hear nothing but his staggered voice
crack open on the cliffs in echo.

   Yet, blinded by the cataract
of his invention, Conan Doyle
can't see the problem isn't final.
Holmes can no more (the public's logic
runs) have perished in those falls
than Falstaff had on the battlefield.
Or had at rough words of Prince Hal's.
Like Shakespeare, who obeyed the queen's
command to resurrect his rascal,
in time the doctor bows to pressure,
dries off his hero, sends him home—
and calls the stories *His Last Bow*.
It's not, of course. Some characters
wake forever in the middle

of their lives: the rooms in Baker Street
are perpetually fixed in place
like letters Holmes speared with a jack-
knife to the mantelpiece; his fiddle
case is never closed.

   Left unsolved: how a B-plus
stylist, Conan Doyle, who preferred
what he called "psychic research," and,
touchingly gullible, obtuse,
finished up his own career
believing in fairies, should have had
the cool to track down the great sleuth
within himself, the cynical
logician who could see in the dark.
Liar, master of disguise,
Holmes elegantly cloaks the thin
transition of two eras: loyal
subject of The Exalted Person
(unnamable Victoria), he's
already prone to modern ills.
Ennui is The Final Problem—for which
there's but a seven percent solution,
or target-practicing indoors
(poor Mrs. Hudson!); with the flair
of one in deep despair, he marks
the whole wall in a manly Braille:
"V.R. done in bullet-pocks."

   How in the world could Conan Doyle
come up with an unkillable myth?
"When you have eliminated all

which is impossible," as Holmes
repeatedly explains, "whatever
remains, however improbable,
must be the truth."

### 3.  *Hearing Shadows*

  President Garfield has been shot,
and Alexander Graham Bell
hops on the train for Washington
to find the bullet. It's lodged somewhere
in the body of the President,
and though he's not a medical man,
Bell hopes to provide a tool.
His "induction balance," as
he calls it, like his "photophone,"
is work that follows in a line
from the telephone—which made his name
six years ago. Disengaged
sometimes from himself, he wonders
if he really *had* invented it.
Or was it someone he'd read about?
That's not a doubt to speak aloud,
with everybody and his brother
daring to claim the patent. "The more
fame a man gets for an invention,"
he once confided to the page,
"the more does he become a target
for the world to shoot at."

The photophone has given him
a synesthetic thrill he's known
only in poetry. (And though
he's far too busy to notice how
he phrases things, that letter to
his father last year was poetry.
"I have been able to hear a shadow,
and even have perceived by ear
the passage of a cloud across
the sun . . .") Insert selenium
in the telephone battery; then throw
light upon it, thus altering
resistance, and varying the strength
of the current sent to the telephone.
An image, then, may have its own
correspondent sound. Simple.

"Watson, come here, I want to see you":
that's all that people can retain,
tending, as people will, to miss
the point. It wasn't just Tom Watson
on the other end of the line,
it was the Telephone in Real
Form he'd wired at last to an
Ideal one floating in his brain.
The question is if he can do
the same again: the deadly ball
sits humming somewhere silently
for his machine to answer it.

He's swept into the White House by
a private entrance. How to enter
the President's body without harm?
He scans the skin with his instrument,
hoping to trigger an alarm.
Three days later, the victim drained
of a once florid cheer, the bullet
like a whole note sings a clear
tone for one measure. Bell returns
to his lab in Massachusetts, fiddles
in vain, more misery intervenes:
his baby boy is born and dies.
Then Garfield does. The autopsy
reveals the bullet had always lain
too deep for a safe extraction—
which hadn't, in fact, been necessary.
A death caused mostly by infection:
doctors' unwashed hands.

    In the history books, poor Garfield
is footnoted for being killed.
But Bell goes on to re-invent
himself, a man who—as he'd said
when the telephone was still afloat—
is lost in fog, and yet can tell
his latitude and longitude.
He takes notes on condensing fresh
water from real fog; conducts
genetic trials on sheep (but fails
to name any of them Dolly); constructs

one flying machine—less like a plane
than a giant paper honeycomb—
after another. "I have not
the shadow of a doubt," he writes
in 1893, "the problem
of aerial navigation will
be solved within ten years." The Wrights
will get there first. But in his way,
as always, he's right on the money.

### 4. *A Tangled Skein*

"'From a drop of water,'" Watson reads
aloud from a magazine, "'a logician
could infer the possibility
of an Atlantic or a Niagara
without having seen or heard of one
or the other.'" He slaps this down
on the table. "What ineffable twaddle!"

It's his first wrong move. The essay's
author, we've foreseen, is Holmes,
his brand-new roommate, about whom
this "Study in Scarlet" proves the first
in scores of chronicles that he—
that is, Dr. Watson—writes.
Dr. Conan Doyle's rough draft
called it "A Tangled Skein." And we
might too, this craft of authorship.

So let them, on my tangling lines,
call the overloaded switchboard
for souls they're linked to, all at once:
Keller and Sullivan, Conan Doyle
and Watson, Bell and Watson, the two
two-watt Watsons, Sullivan
and Watson (either one will do:
all three are listening to this list
and taking notes), Holmes and Watson,
Holmes and his flip side, Moriarty
(not yet heads-first over the falls),
and since the distinction's always fine
between detection and invention,
Holmes and Bell, then Holmes and Bell
(a Dr. Joseph Bell) whom Conan
Doyle had partly modeled Holmes on.

What are they saying? Something about
"the scarlet thread of murder" that runs
"through the colourless skein of life."
That's Holmes—who, in his arrogance
(but no one else can do it right),
kills himself a little with
more cocaine in his scarlet vein.
Something more about resentment
of whatever we have cause to call
ourselves. And yet we'd ask for foils,
for second fiddles, for noble, dim
Watsons as constant witnesses.
Holmes to Watson: "It may be that
you are not yourself luminous . . .
but you are a conductor of light."

Bell to Watson: "Come here, I want
to see you." Holmes to Watson again:
"Come at once if convenient;
if not convenient, come all the same."
And this: "Come, Watson, the game's afoot!"

    And what's the game? Something about
taking a message. A scarlet thread
of reception branches in the brain,
a filament, brilliantly unclear
except for clearly being there—
like the lightbulb waiting to switch on
in the head of half-deaf Edison—
and Conan Doyle is not entirely
wrong, as he joins the conversation,
to add: "I felt that my literary
energies should not be directed
too much into one channel . . ."

    Bell bellows into the phone: "Hurrah!"
(Nobody can ever convince him
to settle for a simple "Hello.")
"Hoy! Hoy!" These days, an older man
embodying an anagram
(as a boy A. Graham Bell had gone
by the alias of "H. A. Largelamb"—
destined, it seems, to experiment
on sheep), he doesn't use the phone
very often anymore. The ring
annoys him at the dinner table;
besides, his wife—the winningly
named Mabel, the original

Ma Bell—is deaf. She writes to us
instead, an essay on the art
of lipreading. A misnomer. The kiss
of unheard word with thought must come,
she says, by marking body clues
(eyebrows, hands); on the lexicon
of context; and, since very little
is ever understood at once,
on empty-headed readiness
to miss a detail. You can feel
your way back to the blanks.

　　Which is the decoding task of Holmes.
The scarlet "Rache" the victim scrawls
on the wall is quickly misconstrued—
if you only read one language—
as "Rachel." But it means revenge.
One letter. What he seeks may hinge
on anything. The dancing men,
a child's line of stick figures, turn
murderous with a hypothesis—
the commonest figure must be "E"—
and Holmes unlocks the cryptogram
so well he tricks the criminal
to present himself for arrest in his
own dancing language: "Come at once."
The flesh made word, the word made flesh.

　　Half-blind Annie Sullivan,
nineteen, untaught, is summoned to
Tuscumbia, Alabama to tame
a child who doesn't know the name

of anything. Then she has a thought.
"I had no idea a short while ago,"
she writes a friend, "how to go to work;
I was feeling about in the dark;
but somehow I know now, and I know
that I know." She's going to pretend,
for now, that Helen understands.
Keep talking. From a drop of water,
a single word, a Niagara
untangles in their hands.

# PART III

# A Kiss in Space

# KANGAROO

Like flustered actors
  who don't know what to do
with their hands, they're hanging
  around in awkward clusters,
paws dangling, ears pricked for a cue.

And then look properly
  stunned when our typecast
tour bus, bumptious as a cousin
  none of them invited, raises
a ruckus of flung stones and dust

and scrapes to a halt
  before them, face to face.
If it isn't clear what a tour bus is,
  they've seen its like before;
their startle softens to a stare

of seeming acceptance,
  as if next time they'd sniff
our coming in advance.  A twitch
  from one, and all's a blank:
in unison they begin to bounce

across the empty
  apron of the plain (where
every line has been forgotten
  or not even thought of once
for millions of years), an unlikely

hop not happy-
  go-lucky but utterly
matter-of-fact; then they stop up-
  stage, for reasons none of us,
on the edge of our seats, can guess.

  Yet it seems so human
    when we happen upon (what
joy, it's blue) a kangaroo
    standing back from the crowd:
her joey's tall enough to nurse

    on its feet, while its head
      and forearms are buried deep
in the pouch, like a woman
    rummaging in her purse for something
nobody else can touch.

# THE SEVEN WEEPERS

The tines of his comb were splitting into finer
brittle strands, like hair, but his own hair—
deader than a corpse's, which can lengthen
in the sweet cool of the coffin—had stopped growing.
Screws unscrewed themselves from wooden boxes
where the stone-dry food was kept. Matches ignited
magically in air, as they fell to earth.
And who would believe it? When he took his pen
to paper, to record the temperature—
a hundred fifty-seven in the sun,
in the shade a hundred thirty-two—the ink
dried at the nib; the lead dropped whole from pencils.
What he had wanted was to draw a line
on the map from Adelaide into the heart
of the outback, where he'd willed a vast Australian
sea like the Caspian. But water holes
of a single shrinking creek were all they'd found,
like the globules of a burst thermometer.

Worst, he thought, was how the rising moon
offered no respite—so blinding that the black
swans that flew across its surface seemed
charred in the passage. Mostly, nothing moved
but ants and lizards. He who had fought
with Wellington against the French, who'd quelled
riots in Ireland, and headed a convict guard
all the way to the wrong end of the world,
where summer raged in January, now
had loitered with his men and bulls and horses
by a nameless pool, with debilitating wisdom,
six months for a drop of rain. In July it came.

And watered them enough to drag themselves
safely for a while across the blank
he named the Stony Desert, with a compass
that couldn't tell them when they should turn back
from infernal sandhills, burnished red, so hard
the horses left no track, as in a dream.
Twice they retrenched and shifted course when hope
of water dried up, shallow and absurd:
a pigeon diving steeply into shadow
that might be mud but wasn't; a clump of bush.
In November a seagull, five hundred miles from sea,
led them to a salt lake, purplish blue,
the color of Heaven.

              What then was this scene
of misery they'd stumbled on? Years later
in England, nearly blind, Charles Sturt would wake
some mornings to that sight of seven naked
black men in a circle by the lake,
wailing and weeping. So profligate! he thought,
spending their grief like that. Who knew
when it would rain again, or if the sun
would bake away this pond of indigo
to nothing? Fools. Better save your tears.

Some in his group knew tribal words, and tried them.
What was the matter? A death? But all the words
were wrong, and the seven weepers seemed

as if they'd long forgotten what it meant
to have an answer. Inconsolable
is all they were. —Somewhere beyond the terror
he'd caused once, early on, in native eyes,
when he'd come bounding forward on his horse.
It wasn't the horse, exactly, but himself
dismounting from it: apparently they'd thought
white man and horse were one, a sort of Centaur.

And yet there were no Centaurs, no such creatures
ever in their heads: the thought now struck him
with the beating of the sun (or so the tale
would go if one retold it as one chose,
too far from 1845 to say
what any of them were) that these were men
wholly unlike himself. What songs they chanted
into the air could only evaporate,
though their chimeras—like the man-sized snake
and the red, preposterous kangaroo—were real.
*Hath the rain a father? Or who hath begotten*
*the drops of dew?* That voice, which thundered now
in the groping cloud of dust that was his mind—
where had it come from?—was of course the voice
of God in the whirlwind, chastising his servant.
And hadn't Job lost seven sons? What help
that fact was to him, he could hardly say,
but he stood there wrapped in silence while the naked
sinners wept, until he could remember

that Job had sat for seven days in silence
before he spoke.

       He didn't have a week
to wait for them; his handkerchief was a rag.
Charles Sturt, whose nation soon would drape its flag
over the weepers' country like a shroud,
reached from his Christian soul and in the heat
uselessly, kindly, gave them his overcoat.

# A Christmas Story

All dressed up in the back
of a taxi stopped at a traffic
light on Central Park West

one cocktail hour in December,
I happened to spot a pair
of shoes dangling in the air—

brown, clownish workshoes dancing
like marionettes from the thick
strings of their knotted laces,

which somebody (with a ladder?)
had flung across the highest
bare bough of a tree.

Tongues out, their eyelets popping,
mimes enacting a desperate
hilarity or disaster,

they reeled, each time a gust
of wind knocked their heads together,
at the naked, shivering business

of living however we must:
possessed, or not, of a clue
as to how it was you lost

first this, then the other shoe
of your one and only pair
(a person who mislays

a pair of shoes on the street
is—paradoxically—not
likely to have a spare);

possessed, or not, of a guess
as to where you should start to look,
or whether the clever soul

who hung your shoes like a star
on a Christmas tree, too far
up to be any use,

had meant to help you out.
Three-faced, the traffic light
turned green and swayed in doubt.

# Institute for the Hand

It feels like jail, or church:
each of us nursing a private pain,
head down, or gazing into space,
inwardly cursing when the search
for gratitude things aren't worse
    steps childishly backward again.

Most of us misstepped
to get here: the architect who tripped
on a railing four inches high, landing
on the hand that was his career,
and tumbling through the universe
    (as in the universal nightmare)

even in his daydreams now,
will fall until his soul's rebuilt;
the first-time mother, a pianist,
who in slipping on the ice had broken
the baby's fall with her own wrist,
    and is consumed by guilt

for daring to mourn it. Yet
what Being begins to care? White-
pawed in outsized plaster, she
suspects that something in us shapes
God in our image. Bad news if we
    are a race evolved from apes.

A hit and run case, brute
injustice on a motorbike
has brought that old man and his wife

(whose hands flew to their faces) here
to undo the crash three times a week
       for the worst stretch of the winter.

       He's mostly cured, I've guessed
from his newly waxed moustache, a touch
unthinkable to the depressed;
but her index finger's locked in that same
wire gizmo, pointing outward as if
       one of us is to blame.

       I look away and pluck
with my good hand a magazine
from the table. What if I stumble on
an exercise routine, or a scene
of skiers afloat on flawless luck?
       (Skiing: that's what did me in.)

       Too risky. I scan my purse
instead for Edgar Allan Poe,
and pry open with my teeth a coffin
for reading glasses—the latest blow
in a series of indignities
       that wound my vanity alone,

       yet seem part of some grand
conspiracy, as if they're *meant*.
In the mystery I turn to, a girl
has been throttled, it appears, by a hand
too mammoth to be human, an agent
       that may be diabolical

or, as Dupin divines, a wild
ex-con that's an orangutang.
A beast with less sense than a child
of motive, or of right and wrong,
whose ideal state is to be jailed,
        whose innocence we can't forgive for long.

# Mr. X

By the time you're forty, you've met so many people
their features fall in place as little bits
from other people, like the Identi-Kits
that victims piece together with the police.
The felon is memory, which takes a face
and slices up what once was very simple.

People you loved, the waiter you saw every week
without seeing, arresting strangers re-assemble
years later in other faces and belong
convincingly there, as if they were unique,
and innocent of how they make you tremble
with remembering or forgetting. I was wrong,

Mr. X—whose cheekbones I recall
from somewhere, and that funny, slightly cross-
eyed, quizzical look you shot me on the sole
occasion we met—to assume you must have lost
someone who looked like me. And yet I stared
longingly at you, as you disappeared.

# COLLAGE

"Garbo," the place is called, but for
some reason, there's an enormous Elvis
above the counter; also some bleak
photographs of Nantucket taken
last summer by a high school senior
whose "collage fund" a presumably
misspelled note invites you to
endow; some bright red gingham place mats
suggesting an Italian motif;
in a somewhat dusty wicker basket,
muffins dense as doorknobs from
the adjoining health food store.

Against one wall, tall thermoses
line up like gas pumps; apparently,
everything's self-service.
Nobody's here, so I help myself
to the House Blend (awful: where's the sugar?)
and open up my paper. A jolly
middle-aged man in a down jacket
emerges from the kitchen. "Got
a bit of a late start this morning,"
he says. "Will you be perfectly comfy
sitting here for three or four minutes
while I step out to buy some cream?"

"Sure will," I answer, with that ready
joshing Americans fall into,
and which shields me from grasping, just
for a moment, what we've said.
Will I be comfy? Will I mind the store?
Will I not be interested in breaking
into the cash register?
Who am I?

—That last question coming from nowhere,
and tilting the room a little. I'm
a stranger who walks into a small
New Hampshire town with a *New York
Times* under her arm, although
she doesn't live in the city either;
somebody whose idea of
reality requires a glance,
over morning coffee, at violence.
Look at this: before they found her dead,
a girl, at her mother's bidding, mopped
the floor with her own head.
A twelve-year-old set a homeless man
afire. And in the inevitable
"positive development,"
they've boarded up a dozen bodegas
that fronted for the drug trade. Will I
be perfectly comfy where the crime
is coffee without cream?

Elvis is still alive and well
on the wall, as the proprietor
returns with two half pints of Half-
and-Half. Think big, I want to tell him;
have one whole idea and carry it through.
But I don't; instead I say, "You must
be proud to live in a town like this,
where everything's run on trust."
Why I should feed him this, in exchange
for such coffee, I can't imagine unless
it's to make *me* feel less strange.

What to do? I pay up feebly
and step out, where overhead the buzz
of a jet is drilling in the reminder
there's nowhere to feel whole, nowhere.
Not even in the sky, where winking
flight attendants are hawking headsets
for the movie promised after lunch—
this month, "The Last of the Mohicans,"
where stealthily, in moccasins
or boots, people on little screens
hack each other to bits.

# Absolute September

How hard it is to take September
straight—not as a harbinger
of something harder.

Merely like suds in the air, cool scent
scrubbed clean of meaning—or innocent
of the cold thing coldly meant.

How hard the heart tugs at the end
of summer, and longs to haul it in
when it flies out of hand

at the prompting of the first mild breeze.
It leaves us by degrees
only, but for one who sees

summer as an absolute,
Pure State of Light and Heat, the height
to which one cannot raise a doubt,

as soon as one leaf's off the tree
no day following can fall free
of the drift of melancholy.

# Marco Polo

Midafternoon, and both shades drawn
over open windows: the September sun,
bright but temperate, is diffused
as through a lantern. My child and I
are lying on top of the covers, reading.
She has her book and I have mine.

She can read silently. So I can't
say what's happening in her book,
or how far it takes her from our narrow
New England street where, days from now,
a yellow school bus will rumble back
to claim her. But the noise out there

at this moment—the grating of roller skates
and of other children's voices (*Marco
Polo! Marco Polo!*) clearly
doesn't enter her ears at all.
In my book, set in old Tennessee, the author—
or the narrator at least—seems to feel

that the lazy lineages of his tale,
the burials, marriages, repay
our interest just because family
is always interesting. And because
he thinks so he's right; or that's partly why.
Thinking so makes him write that way:

some clumsy scandal or other is nobler
simply by having been described
in clean, smooth blocks of paragraphs,

well-paced, well-chosen words, and with
an even-handedness we wish
we rose to, in life, more than fleetingly.

A breeze through the pair of windows turns
one of the shades up like a page,
then the other. Nothing makes her stir,
little reader. I'm no match for her.
I find I'm picturing the blind-
folded boy on the street, his arms outstretched

for the bodies of voices (*Marco Polo!*
*Marco Polo!*) that circle and taunt him,
and though it's only a game, the sounds
drift to my windows with the heightened
importance of the half-understood.
My book hasn't lost me, exactly; it seems

it's succeeding in leading me away
from itself—as a parent does, or tries to—
with something of its tone in my head.
I've never loved her more than today.
Why this should be, or how long joy
is containable, or how far she'll travel

to shake me—all of this matters, but
I manage not to say it aloud;
following the thought, the room
darkens when the schoolday sun,
as if trying on a new jacket, slips
briefly into a cloud.

# AU PAIR

The first thing she'd noticed, as they sat her down for lunch
by the picture window, was flags all doing a dance
in front of houses: was today a holiday?
No, they said smiling, it's just the American way,
and she couldn't help reflecting that in France
nobody needed reminding they were French,

but the neighborhood had turned out very nice,
no fences, big yards, kids racing back and forth;
you could let the shower run while you were soaping
or get ice from a giant refrigerator's face.
She couldn't believe how much the franc was worth
and she had no boyfriend yet, but she was hoping,

and because her father was the world's best baker
she naturally thought of his bakery in the Alps
whenever they passed her a slice of their so-called bread,
and sometimes she wished she could hire a jet to take her
back just for breakfast, but as her great-aunt had said
so wisely more than once, it never helps

to make comparisons, so she mostly refrained.
She couldn't believe, though, how here whenever it rained
the mother sent children out without their coats,
not carelessly, but because she had no power
and nobody made them finish the food on their plates
and bedtime was always bedtime plus an hour,

so au pairs were useless really, except for the driving.
Yes, that was puzzling: after she cracked up the car
they didn't blame her or ask her to pay a thing,
but once she let Caitlin eat some sort of cherry
with red dye in it, and then they *were* angry, very.
Americans were strange, that much was clear:

no penmanship, and lesbians held hands
on the street, and most women carried a pair
of pumps in a bag they never took out to wear;
it was so disrespectful, she couldn't understand
how older ones got called nothing, not even Madame,
but then nobody in this country had a last name

which was going to make it hard to write them a letter
when she got back.  It was really bittersweet
her visa was running out; she was sad that all
she'd done with her days off was go to the mall,
she'd bought a million T-shirts and that was great
but she had to admit it, saving would have been better,

and she knew somehow that when she got on the plane
she'd probably never live anywhere foreign again
which filled her American family with more pity
than she felt for herself, because at least she was coping,
she'd work at her sister's shop and stay in the city
where she had no boyfriend yet.  But she was hoping.

# A Robin's Nest

Of the four fuchsia plants that hung
over the porch (the drooping
neck on every stem so heavy
with jeweled blooms they lost

all sense of posture), who's to say
what called one to a function other
than merely growing? Watering
the fourth one afternoon, I found

coiled within the elemental
circle of the plastic planter
a rustic imitation: the woven
ribbons of a robin's nest.

A perfect fit, like the band inside
the crown of a hat! And then the straw
of the nest itself became a hat—
a pillbox fortress, hardier

and taller all day long, because
of some law of nature whereby theft
is always rewarded. Ripping off
from trees these wisps of bark, as if

robbing Peter to pay Paul,
the bird would have the potted soil
as well—and so persuaded me
never to water it. I saw the eggs

a few days later, a four-eyed stare
of childish, uncomprehending blue—
lucky, like a four-leafed clover.
And then (but why the surprise?) the peep

of fluff above the top one morning,
like the stuffing of a padded
envelope torn open, and though
I read the message at a respectful

distance, even the fuzzy print
was easy to decipher. While
the vines were nearly dead, four buds
(less like the fuchsia's than a snap-

dragon's that never snapped) flung back
their heads on funny rubber necks,
beaks open in a parody
of ecstasy. And through the air

she swooped to them who couldn't see
what they'd been longing for—the tender
worm that streamed like a banner from
her beak, the lifted battle flag

of life's own bloody victory.

# LIAM

He's down again, aswim in a dream
of milk, and Teresa who is far
too tired to go back to sleep goes back
to the table where she tests the nib
of her pen, like the nipple on a bottle.

Into a bottle of permanent ink
she dips her pen and begins to trace
over her pencil-marks on the face
of the spiral scrapbook the name they chose
for him who has never dreamed of a name.

It's *William,* like his father, but
she has only got as far as *Will*
(the doubled *l* another spiral
to the *Liam* they now call him), which
leaves her still three letters to spell

the man who's curled up in *I am.*
—The stranger in the crib who seems
longer each time they lift him out
and will find that while they named the story
it is his to write.

# A KISS IN SPACE

That the picture
  in *The Times* is a blur
    is itself an accuracy. Where
this has happened is so remote
    that clarity would misrepresent
not only distance but our feeling
    about distance: just as
the first listeners at the telephone
    were somehow reassured to hear
static that interfered with hearing
    (funny word, *static*, that conveys
the atom's restlessness), we're
    not even now—at the far end
of the century—entirely ready
    to look to satellites for mere

    resolution. When the *Mir*
      invited the first American
        astronaut to swim in the pool
of knowledge with Russians, he floated
    exactly as he would have in space
stations of our own: no lane
    to stay in, no line to determine
the deep end, Norman Thagard
    hovered on the ceiling something
like an angel in a painting
    (but done without the hard
outlines of Botticelli; more
    like a seraph's sonogram),
and turned to Yelena Kondakova
    as his cheek received her kiss.

And in this
　　too the blur made sense: a kiss
　　so grave but gravity-free, untouched
by Eros but nevertheless
　　out of the usual orbit, must
make a heart shift focus. The very
　　grounding in culture (they gave him bread
and salt, as Grandmother would a guest
　　at her dacha; and hung the Stars
and Stripes in a stiff crumple
　　because it would not fall), the very
Russianness of the bear hugs was
　　dizzily universal: for who
knows how to signal anything
　　new without a ritual?

　　Not the kitchen-table
　　reader (child of the Cold War,
　　of 3 x 5 cards, carbon copies,
and the manila folder), who takes a pair
　　of scissors—as we do when the size
of some idea surprises—and clips
　　this one into a rectangle
much like her piece of toast. There:
　　it's saved, to think of later.
Yet it would be unfair
　　to leave her looking smug; barely
a teenager when she watched, on
　　her snowy TV screen, a man
seeming to walk on the moon, she's
　　learned that some detail—

Virtual Reality or e-mail,
　　something inexplicable and
　　unnatural—is always cropping up
for incorporation in what's human.
　　What ought to make it manageable,
and doesn't quite, is the thought
　　of humans devising it. She'll
remember Norman Thagard in June,
　　when the *Mir* (meaning Peace: but how
imagine this without agitation?)
　　docks with the *Atlantis* (meaning
the island Plato mentioned first
　　and which, like him, did not disappear
without a splash), to shuttle
　　the traveler back home—or

　　　　to whatever Earth has become.

# Notes and Acknowledgments

A NOTE ON SOURCES for some of the poems: "Alternating Currents" was born from a remark by the playwright Suzan-Lori Parks that both Sherlock Holmes and Alexander Graham Bell had assistants named Watson. The most useful books I consulted for the poem included *Bell: Alexander Graham Bell and the Conquest of Solitude,* by Robert V. Bruce; *The Complete Sherlock Holmes,* by Sir Arthur Conan Doyle (and the preface by Christopher Morley in the two-volume Doubleday edition); Helen Keller's *The Story of My Life, with her letters (1887–1901) and a supplementary account of her education, including passages from the reports and letters of her teacher, Anne Mansfield Sullivan, by John Albert Macy,* and her subsequent autobiography, *Midstream: My Later Life; Helen and Teacher: The Story of Helen Keller and Anne Sullivan Macy,* by Joseph Lash; *Alexander Graham Bell: The Man Who Contracted Space,* by Catherine MacKenzie; *Naked Is the Best Disguise: The Death and Resurrection of Sherlock Holmes,* by Samuel Rosenberg; and *Conan Doyle: Portrait of an Artist,* by Julian Symons. (Quotations from these books are at times altered by a syllable or two for poetic purposes. Events are occasionally reordered or conflated. My descriptions of Bell's inventions oversimplify, and are probably highly unscientific.) "The Seven Weepers" is based on Charles Sturt's travels in Australia as recorded in Alan Moorehead's book *Cooper's Creek*, though the excursion into the Book of Job is mine.

Several residencies at the MacDowell Colony aided me enormously in writing this book. I am also deeply grateful for a year in Paris as the Amy Lowell Poetry Travelling Scholar.

Some dedications: "Fire-Breathing Dragon" to William and Wendy Garner; "A Rainbow over the Seine" to Emily Lodge; "A Leak Somewhere" to Albert and Janet Salter; "Video Blues" to Brad Leithauser; "Brief Candle" to Gladys Leithauser and Arthur Higbee; "A Magnet" to Alfred Corn, whose own poem "Self-Portrait with Refrigerator Magnets" inspired it; "A Swing" to Jacques Bonnet; "Home Movies: A Sort of Ode" to Madeleine Blais; "Libretto" to Daniel Hall; "Sound Effects" to Jon Stallworthy, whose insights and imagery in *Louis MacNeice: A Biography* I made use of; "Cutlery" and "The Jewel of the World" to Peggy O'Shea; "Hail in Honfleur" to Ann Close; "Distance" to Cynthia Zarin; "Kangaroo" to Paul Kane; "The Seven Weepers" to Peter Rose; "A Christmas Story" to Ann Hulbert; "Institute for the Hand" to Joe Phillips; "Mr. X" to Peggy O'Brien; "Collage" to Marty Townsend; "Marco Polo" to Hilary Leithauser; "Au Pair" to Nancy Kundl; "A Robin's Nest" to Emily Leithauser; "Liam" to Liam Salter; "A Kiss in Space" to Anthony and Helen Hecht. "Wreckage" and "Absolute September" were dedicated to James Merrill in a memorial tribute in *Verse*.

My husband, Brad Leithauser, helped me every step of the way.

*A Note About the Author*

Mary Jo Salter grew up in Detroit and Baltimore, and was educated at Harvard and at Cambridge University. She is the author of three previous collections of poems, *Henry Purcell in Japan* (1985), *Unfinished Painting* (1989, the Lamont Selection for the year's most distinguished second volume of poetry), and *Sunday Skaters* (1994), as well as a children's book, *The Moon Comes Home* (1989). She is also an editor of *The Norton Anthology of Poetry*.

Her many awards include the Witter Bynner Prize and fellowships from the National Endowment for the Arts, the Guggenheim Foundation, the Ingram Merrill Foundation, and the Amy Lowell Trust. An Emily Dickinson Lecturer in the Humanities at Mount Holyoke College, she lives in South Hadley, Massachusetts, with her husband, the writer Brad Leithauser, and their daughters, Emily and Hilary.

## A Note on the Type

This book was set in Fairfield, the first typeface from the hand of the distinguished American artist and engraver Rudolph Ruzicka (1883–1978). In its structure Fairfield displays the sober and sane qualities of the master craftsman whose talent has long been dedicated to clarity. It is this trait that accounts for the trim grace and vigor, the spirited design and sensitive balance, of this original typeface.

Rudolph Ruzicka was born in Bohemia and came to America in 1894. He set up his own shop, devoted to wood engraving and printing, in New York in 1913 after a varied career working as a wood engraver, in photoengraving and banknote printing plants, and as an art director and freelance artist. He designed and illustrated many books, and was the creator of a considerable list of individual prints—wood engravings, line engravings on copper, and aquatints.

*Composed by NK Graphics,*
*Keene, New Hampshire*

*Printed by The Stinehour Press,*
*Lunenburg, Vermont*

*Bound by Quebecor Printing,*
*Brattleboro, Vermont*

*Designed by Cassandra J. Pappas*